THE TRAUMA
OF
BEING BLACK
BY
ELIMENE MERIZIER

DISCLAIMER:

The views and opinions expressed in this book are solely that of the author. The experiences and observations of the author are not encompassing of all traumas that **Black** Americans go through nor am I speaking for all **blacks**.

DEDICATION

This book is dedicated to my beautiful, funny, smart, dark chocolate daughter, Nadia. Don't ever dim your light for anyone and always remember that you are powerful beyond imagination. You're such a talented, resilient, assertive, smart, innovative, and loving girl. You are a force to be reckoned with and I am so proud and thankful that God blessed me to be your mother.

To Marquis, the man of my dreams and my knight in shining armor. You came into my life and swept me off my feet. My love and desire for you are indescribable. Your presence in my life has been truly a Godsend and I am so very thankful for you. In the words of Anthony Hamilton, "the point of it all, is I love you".

To one of my closest friends, Brittaney. I love our conversations, your tenacity, drive, and spirit. I can't wait to see the great things that you will accomplish and the lives that you will touch.

I also want to thank God for the inspiration, the gift of writing, and the talents that He has given to me to share with the world. God does not make mistakes, so even knowing the hurt and pain that we as humans would bring upon each other, He still created us and loves us no matter what. I have to give thanks for the trials and tribulations that He has brought me through and will continue to do. May God's blessings and grace be upon you, my dear reader.

TABLE OF CONTENTS

INTRODUCTION

Congratulations on making the first step towards acknowledging **Black** Trauma. If you have not experienced **Black** Trauma, based on the title of the book, the assumption is that it piqued your interest enough to learn about it. While you may not be familiar with the term yet, after reading this book I hope you will have a better understanding of **Black** Trauma. As you read through these pages, I ask that you have an open mind, try to empathize, and reflect on what you read.

The point of this book is to give insight into the trauma that **Blacks** go through consistently in America. Many others may see the trauma but choose to turn a blind eye and choose to remain ignorant, which is a privilege. I hope that this book will enlighten the reader, but know that there is no expectation for the reader to fully understand the trauma if they have never experienced it before.

Writing this book was therapeutic because it provided an outlet to express the frustrations and write about the absolute absurdities that **blacks** often experience. For those who have adopted, are raising **black c**hildren, or have biracial children, I hope that this book will provide some insight into things that they may experience. Please understand that having a non-black family does not shield, protect, or block your child from experiencing racism. It also does not give a pass to not discuss racism openly and honestly to the best of your ability, because doing so does more damage to the child than you may realize or understand.

For other **blacks** who choose to read this, I want you

to know that your feelings are validated, your trauma is validated, your experiences are validated, and you are valued. Your life matters. You matter. Stay strong. Stay true to yourself. Raise your sons and daughters to be proud **black** boys and **black** girls. There is no shame in being proud of who you are and who God created you to be.

RACIAL TRAUMA

According to Mental Health America, racial trauma is the emotional and mental injury caused by racially biased encounters, ethnic discrimination, hate crimes, and outright racism. Racial trauma is also known as race-based traumatic stress and can present symptoms similar to that of post-traumatic stress disorder and any individual who is subjected to a racist encounter is at a risk for suffering from race-based traumatic stress. Mental Health America notes that in the United States, **Black** Indigenous People of Color are the most vulnerable to experience racial trauma due to "living under a system of white supremacy". Furthermore, Comas-Díaz et al. (2019), noted the repeated exposure to race-based stress that minority individuals and groups experience is similar to post-traumatic stress disorder. The caveat is that race-based trauma stress is disregarded as a mental health disorder and is, instead, considered a mental injury (Mental Health America, n.d.). The issue with this classification is that while the symptoms presented, as noted above are akin to post-traumatic stress disorder, the trauma is continually happening in the present. The usage of the term "mental injury" presents the issue of race-based traumatic stress as something that is minor and can simply be healed. On the other hand, a mental disorder has conditions that impact behavior, thinking, mood, feelings, and can be chronic along with affecting one's ability to properly function and interact with others (Medline Plus, n.d.). As one can see, there is a significant difference in the understanding of race-trauma as a mental injury versus a mental disorder. The mental injury definition does not give credence to the severity of racism and its impact on those who experience it.

Based on this author's experience with racism as a **black** person and a **black** woman, the practice of grouping all races into the category of "racial trauma" and "race-based trauma" diminishes the extent of the trauma that **Black** Americans encounter. While other minorities may experience trauma from racism and discrimination, I believe that **blacks** sustain a distinctly different trauma and there needs to be a clear separation between racial trauma as a general label for all races and the trauma that **blacks** face. This author identifies it as **Black** Trauma and there are examples of this trauma provided later on in this book. Understand that trauma has been imposed on **blacks** in America since our ancestors were forcefully brought to this country to be slaves. Psychological trauma was inflicted upon slaves as a means of instilling fear and establishing mental bondage, which is still evident in the **black** community today. Some examples of the psychological trauma that **black** slaves had to endure can be found in *The Willie Lynch Letter: The Making of a Slave*. It has been said that this book was derived from a speech given by Willie Lynch, a British slave owner in the West Indies, to the slave owners in the Colony of Virginia in 1712. Much of what has manifested in the **black** community can be attributed to the trauma that was imposed on our ancestors, which has created a perpetual cycle of self-destruction. As you read on, you will have the opportunity to read some of the passages from the letter, but for now we will look at some examples of the trauma of being **black**.

THE TRAUMA OF BEING BLACK

The trauma of being **black** is being invisible part of the time and being seen as a threat the other part. Don't believe me? Ask the "proverbial scary" **black** man.

The trauma of being **black** is that when we say "**black** life matters" the inevitable response is "yea, but..."

The trauma of being **black** is that a wall has more value than a **black** life, as portrayed in the case of Breonna Taylor.

The trauma of being **black** is that when there are discussions on racial issues the speaker is inevitably the representative voice for all **blacks**, especially when the speaker opposes other **blacks'** views on racial issues. These particular "representatives" are purposefully sought out to discredit all other **blacks** because they fit the agenda of the opposers. We are individuals.

The trauma of being **black** is that history has been spun to conveniently leave out the truth. An example of this is that the

Black Panther Party, when discussed, was a "terrorist" group. The reality is that they formed to protect **blacks** from police brutality, started the free breakfast program, and opened free health clinics in **black** communities across the United States (History.com, 2019).

The trauma of being **black** is that the "War on Drugs" was just another tactic to slim down the **black** population and intentionally separate **black** and Latino families. The arrest and high incarceration rates are not due to increased drug use, but law enforcement targeting urban, low-income areas (Drug Policy Alliance, n.d.).

The trauma of being **black** is the White House, built on the backs of **blacks**, was probably never intended for or imagined that there would ever be a **black** president one day.

The trauma of being **black** is that **blacks** are often used as test subjects for various diseases and illnesses.

The trauma of being **black** is that our government bombed and massacred entire cities of thriving **blacks** in Tulsa, Oklahoma; West Philadelphia, Pennsylvania; Wilmington, North Carolina; and Seneca Village, New York, and many more cities, yet conveniently leave those truths out of history books.

The trauma of being **black** is not having the privilege to just <u>exist</u>.

The trauma of being **black** is that jogging, walking, driving, or just plain being **black** can be a death sentence without a trial, a judge, or a jury.

The trauma of being **black** is that freedom is not extended to all even while living in the "land of the free".

The trauma of being **black** is that our healthcare is less than sub-par and **black** women have the highest rate of dying during or after childbirth, even in 2020.

The trauma of being **black** is having to stay calm at all times, lest someone mistakes us for the "angry **black** woman" or the "scary **black** man".

The trauma of being **black** is being silenced.

The trauma of being **black** is only being loved for our talents, but not as a people, or who we are as individuals. Case in point: Look how people reacted over Kobe Bryant dying but had and still have, an insatiable hatred for George Floyd. The hatred was evident while he lay with a knee to his neck being murdered in front of the world. They were both **black** men who died, except George Floyd was not a valued member of society so his death was "acceptable" in the eyes of too many people.

The trauma of being **black** is the "you're pretty for a **black** girl" microaggressive compliments, or "you speak so proper", or "you talk like a white girl", or "wow, you can pronounce and enunciate all syllables of your words" statements.

The trauma of being **black** is having to constantly fight that my life matters and it is beyond exasperating.

The trauma of being **black** is that others emulate us when things are good, but quickly exit stage left, right, and center when things get too real. That is privilege.

The trauma of being **black** is the anxiety when a cop pulls us over because an alleged taillight out could very well be the last taillight ever.

The trauma of being **black** is the fear of having children because once they are out of the "cute" stage, they are officially viewed as a threat and treated as a deadly weapon.

The trauma of being **black** is hearing or reading the ignorant comments when one of us is murdered by law enforcement. The collective thought is that "they shouldn't have been resisting arrest or being threatening".

The trauma of being **black** is that running AWAY and getting shot in the back is considered resisting arrest.

The trauma of being **black** is that there are multiple videos of non-blacks <u>shooting</u> at the police, <u>fighting</u> them, and <u>legitimately resisting arrest</u>, yet are still <u>alive</u> today with their actions written off as them "not handling stress very well". This equates to saying, "if they weren't **black**, they'd still be alive".

The trauma of being **black** is having to have conversations with our children that their lives are legitimately in danger BECAUSE of their skin color. That their father, uncles, cousins, brothers, friends, aunts, mother, and sisters could be gunned down with no repercussions when it is law enforcement or "vigilantes".

The trauma of being **black** is the fear that when 911 is called, the responding officers are prepared to end your life rather than protect it.

The trauma of being **black** is being just as educated or more than our non-black counterparts and still not be good enough.

The trauma of being **black** is not knowing a native language, ancestral roots, or our true names because they were forcefully stripped away and replaced. In his speech, Willie Lynch, detailed annihilating the "mother tongue" and instituting a new language as a way to break the **black** slave (Lynch, 1712/2017).

 The trauma of being **black** is being hated by our own on top of the hate from others. Lynch (1712/2017) taught other slave owners to cause discord amongst the slaves. He did this by pitting the old **black** males against the young **black** males, dark skin versus light skin, light skin versus dark skin, coarse hair versus fine hair, plantation status, and much more to create perpetual distrust and internal hatred within the **black** community that is still prevalent today.

The trauma of being **black** is being too dark, too light, too nappy, too proper, too hood, too ghetto, or just too **black**.

The trauma of being **black** is having to specify "African American" in web searches to find representation that looks like us, has similar hair, or find products that will actually work for us.

The trauma of being **black** is being broken emotionally, physically, mentally, and spiritually, while being force-fed another culture with the intent to keep us in the dark about our own cultures. Similar to this, Lynch (1712/2017) used the same principles for breaking horses to break the slave. He noted that reducing them (**blacks**) from their natural state in nature where they are independent to create a dependency where we (slave owners) may get useful production for business and pleasure.

◆ ◆ ◆

The trauma of being **black** is being seen as a scary superhuman and less than a human at the same time.

◆ ◆ ◆

The trauma of being **black** is the lasting insecurities and/or the self-hatred imposed from a young age due to treatment based on skin color.

◆ ◆ ◆

The trauma of being **black** is the terror lynchings that were family outings, advertised in the newspapers, used on postcards sent to friends and family as proof of the joyous family fun and the true meaning behind "picnics". Researchers at the Equal Justice Initiative acknowledged that racial terror lynching was more prevalent than what was previously reported. Racial terror lynching was used to enforce racial segregation and Jim Crow laws to maintain control by victimizing **black** Americans.

The trauma of being **black** is not having the privilege to turn a blind eye, claim ignorance, or offer an empty apology only after being pressured into it.

The trauma of being **black** is that there is no gray area and no margin of error.

The trauma of being **black** is that having a mental health crisis during a "well-being check" by law enforcement can be a death sentence. See the irony?

The trauma of being **black** is having to suppress our emotions lest they be too overwhelming for others.

The trauma of being **black** is that whenever a law enforcement officer kills a **black** man, the first thing people do is look up the victim's criminal history to justify them being murdered.

The trauma of being **black** is that the rage we feel from centuries upon centuries of suppression and oppression has been invalidated and we are told to "get over it".

The trauma of being **black** is that talking about racial issues is "taboo" and makes others "too uncomfortable", so it goes unaddressed.

The trauma of being **black** is having to smile and remain calm even when anger is more than justified.

The trauma of being **black** is that every time there is a death at the hands of law enforcement, the consensus is that our focus should be on stopping all the "**black** on **black**" crime.

The trauma of being **black** is that "**black** on **black**" crime is a made up offense to further the propaganda that **blacks** are violent and scary. Mock (2015) pointed out that "**black**-on-**black** violence" is a by-product of concentrated poverty and racial segregation. Further noted is that **black** offenders do not kill others or commit crimes against other **blacks** solely because they have dark skin, as a Klansman would do (Mock, 2015). The crimes committed by **blacks** against other **blacks** are often due to proximity and opportunity with the understanding that they will likely get away with the crime. For example, if a **black** person commits a crime in a **black** neighborhood, outside of those affected, no one really cares. So long as the crime is not committed in a predominately white neighborhood, most crimes never make the news, unless it is being used to perpetuate the fear of **black**. Mock (2015) noted that African American and **Black** communities have been robbed and plundered by real estate developers for decades, yet it is not considered a "white- on- **black**" crime. Whites kill other whites, yet their crimes are not documented as "white-on-white" crimes. Same for Asian, Hispanic, and other offenders. The evidence lies in the deep-rooted hatred for **blacks** in America.

The trauma of being **black** is the justification of the use of the N-word by non-blacks because "my best friend is **black**", or "I'm married to a **black** man or **black** woman", or "my kid is **black**".

The trauma of being **black** is that one person's viewpoint or opinion is blanketly applied to all **blacks**.

The trauma of being **black** is that even if you were raised in a non-black community or household, you are still not immune to racism.

The trauma of being **black** is that our **black** men have to alter their behavior to not be deemed as "scary" or "menacing".

The trauma of being **black** is that we can be falsely accused of a crime and be either gunned down or erroneously imprisoned over it with no repercussions for the false reporter.

The trauma of being **black** is that **black** men make up the largest percentage of inmates at 38.6% (Federal Bureau of Prisons, 2021), even though they only make up less than 7% of the United States population (US Census Bureau, 2019). The overall rates of incarceration of **blacks** (1,408/100,000) compared to whites (275/100,000) and Hispanics (378/100,000) shows that **blacks** are over five times more likely to be incarcerated than their white counterparts (Nellis, 2016).

◆ ◆ ◆

The trauma of being **black** is that a "jury of your peers" is never that. One of many examples of this is the case of Curtis Flowers who was on trial for capital murder in the state of Mississippi. The Mississippi District Attorney's office prosecuted him six times, striking almost all the **black** jurors each time (Death Penalty Information Center, 2018).

◆ ◆ ◆

The trauma of being **black** is the assumption that only the **black** person could be offended by a racist joke, a post with racist content, or a racist comment.

◆ ◆ ◆

The trauma of being **black** is serving in the Air Force for over ten years and experiencing firsthand the "persistent and consistent racial bias against **black** Airmen" (Vanden Brook, 2020), yet the Air Force only openly acknowledged racial bias in May of 2020.

◆ ◆ ◆

The trauma of being black is that being black is not a choice. "Blue lives matter" and "All Lives Matter" were counter-arguments against "**Black** Lives Matter". However, after the riots that occurred at the Capitol Building on January 6th, 2021, it became quite evident that "All Lives" and "Blue Lives" really did not matter and was only used to overshadow and deflect from the injustices that **blacks** experience in the United States. Being **black** is not a simple career choice or a choice in general. It is our life.

THE WILLIE LYNCH LETTER AND THE MAKING OF A SLAVE

I have read the Willie Lynch Letter multiple times and often use it as a teaching tool when I teach my finance courses, "Breaking the Poverty Mentality". Some may not understand the importance of this letter and how it has greatly impacted the **black** community. Lynch (1712/2017) wrote that if the slave owners in the Colony of Virginia followed his instructions correctly that it will control the slaves "for at least 300 years". I use this quote because many in the **black** community still embody the slave mentality. The slave mentality correlates to a mindset where one remains in bondage while being physically free. It manifests as envy, jealousy, and hatred even though the desire for better is there, the result is that one is content with complaining about their situation and shaming others for their drive. Some slaves chose slavery over freedom and though modern-day **blacks** are "free", there are many who are still in a state of perpetual bondage. To be clear, while the example was used to explain the slave mentality in the **black** community, keep in mind that this mentality exists outside the **black** community as well.

As evidenced in "The Making of a Slave", some of the slave owners were truly sadistic. Lynch (1712/2017) instructed slave owners to take the meanest, most restless slave and strip him in front of the other male, female, and child slaves. Then tar and feather him and tie each leg to horses facing opposite directions, set fire to him, then beat both horses so that they pull him apart in front of the slaves. Other male slaves were beaten to the point of death in front of the female slaves and children to instill fear and cause psychological trauma (Lynch, 1712/2017). After they stripped the males of their dignity, the female was stripped of hers by being beat into submission so that she could train her offspring to be submissive as well. Along with the beatings and other physical punishments, Willie Lynch instructed slave owners to break the female slaves' dependency on their male counterparts by forcing her to watch as the males were beaten almost to death to give her the sense of being alone and unprotected because the male image was destroyed (Lynch, 1712/2017). The intent of this was two-fold: create a psychological independent state in the female slave and create a submissive dependent state of mind for the male slaves. By reversing the male and female roles, Lynch (1712/2017) noted that they "created an orbiting cycle" turning on its own axis unless a "phenomenon re-shifts the positions".

The irrational and seemingly innate fear of the **black** male often leads to their untimely demise at the hands of self-appointed "vigilantes" and trigger-happy law enforcement officers. It is crazy that the **black** man is feared so much by white counterparts without legitimate cause, but on the flip side, **black** males have every reason to be fearful of whites due to a history of serious harm and/or death at the hands of them. Emmet Till is evidence that a **black** man or child could be brutally terrorized and lynched simply over the false allegation of a white woman. To this day Carolyn Bryant, his accuser, has not faced any repercussions for her role in his death. Carolyn Bryant waited until she was 72 years old before confessing that she lied about Emmet Till (Equal Justice Initiative, 2017). She played a direct role in his lynching, yet has lived a life of privilege while his life was cut short, solely because of her. We can take this example to lead us into a discussion on the roles that victims can play in their victimization and how being victimized has impacted the **black** community.

VICTIMOLOGY, **BLACK** TRAUMA, AND THE PSYCHOLOGICAL DAMAGE

Does a victim play a part in their victimization? How does one become a victim? How has victimization affected the **black** community? To answer those questions, we will first examine what Victimology is. Victimology is the scientific study of victimization that includes studying the relationship between offenders and victims, investigators, the court system, media, corrections, and social movements (Science Direct, 2014). The pioneer of victim typography was Benjamin Mendelsohn, who categorized victims of crime to better understand victimization. Sanchez (n.d.) noted that Mendelsohn emphasized the victim's role and attitude in becoming a victim. According to Mendelsohn's Typology of Crime Victims, there are six types of victims including the victim with minor guilt, completely innocent victim, victim as guilty as the offender (voluntary victim), victim more guilty than the offender (instigator), most guilty victim, and the imaginary victim (SAGE, 2016).

The first victim type that will be discussed is the Imaginary Victim. This particular victim is someone who pretends to be a victim and will falsely report their "victimization" in hopes of getting their way or showing their privilege. We saw this type of victim emerge in full force this past year in the rise of the "Karen". As evidenced over the past year, the "Karen" is one who takes pride in making themselves into a victim by inserting themselves in situations where they have no rhyme or reason for being there. This often involves needing to speak to a manager about a perceived injustice done to them. When the "injustice" involves another race, they are irrationally fearful for their lives and will use that as a means of getting law enforcement to respond faster. The "Karen" will display their victim status by calling law enforcement on members of other races for doing normal activities, such as working, spending time with their family, barbequing, getting into their vehicles, living in the same neighborhood, or just plain existing.

Another example of the Imaginary Victim is the case of Amber Guyger murdering Botham Jean on September 6, 2018. Amber Guyger became an Imaginary Victim when she murdered Botham Jean after allegedly mistaking his apartment for hers and thinking he was an intruder. What is interesting about one of the testimonies in this case is that the lead homicide investigator, Texas Ranger David Armstrong, testified without the jury that he did not believe Guyger had committed a crime because it was "reasonable for her to perceive him (Botham Jean) as a deadly threat" (Hutchinson, 2019). The **black** man has always been seen as a deadly threat to the white man and white woman. One of the issues in this case is that Botham Jean was eating ice cream and playing video games in his apartment, yet was seen as a deadly threat by someone breaking and entering into HIS APARTMENT. Do you see the absurdity?

Another example of **blacks** seen as a deadly threat is the case of Tamir Rice, who was twelve years old when he was murdered by Cleveland Police Officers Timothy Loehmann and Frank Garmback. Tamir Rice was playing with a toy airsoft pistol when an individual called 911 to report a "guy with a pistol". The 911 caller provided detailed information that the person with the gun was "probably a juvenile" with a gun that was "probably fake", but described the situation as "very frightening" (Department of Justice, 2020). The emergency dispatcher broadcast the call as a high priority call, and relayed to the responding officers that there was a "**black** male sitting on the swing wearing a camouflage hat, gray jacket with black sleeves, and keeps pulling a gun out of his pants and pointing it at people" (Department of Justice, 2020). The dispatcher (conveniently) failed to pass on the information that the individual they will encounter may be a juvenile with a toy gun. Due to this failure to communicate all aspects about the person of interest, the responding officers were primed and ready to face a "deadly threat" and this is exactly what happened. Within seconds of arriving at the playground and "confronting" Tamir Rice, Officer Loehmann fired two shots that killed him. Neither of the officers was indicted and only faced administrative punishments.

The next victim typology is the Guilty Victim. This particular victim may have instigated the conflict but is killed or injured by the victim in self-defense. This type of victim is often seen in domestic violence-related situations, however, the victim is often punished as seen in the cases of Marissa Alexander, Cyntoia Brown, Eisha Love, and Bresha Medows to name a few.

The third and last type of victim that we will discuss is the victim with minor guilt. This type of victim was portrayed in the George Floyd case that was the literal tipping point in the (mis)treatment of **blacks** in America. On May 25th, 2020 police in Minneapolis were called after an employee at a convenience store called 911 to report that Mr. Floyd had purchased some cigarettes with a possibly counterfeit $20 bill. After receiving the call, Officer Thomas Lane approached the car Mr. Floyd was sitting in with two other people and immediately drew his weapon and pulled George Floyd from the car, to which Officer Lane reports as him "actively resisted being handcuffed". In case you missed it, the responding officer did not explain why he was handcuffing Mr. Floyd until after he was handcuffed. According to body cameras, Mr. Floyd appears to be cooperative from the beginning of the arrest and even repeatedly apologized to the officers after they approached his car. After repeatedly asking Mr. Floyd to show his hands, the officers tried to put Mr. Floyd in the squad car and this is when a struggle occurred. Mr. Floyd told officers he was claustrophobic. Now on the scene is Officer Derek Chauvin who attempts to assist with getting Mr. Floyd in the vehicle. Officer Chauvin pulled Mr. Floyd away from the passenger side of the vehicle which caused him to fall to the ground. The officers allowed Mr. Floyd to lay on the ground, handcuffed, and face down. While still restrained, Officer Chauvin made the conscious decision to kneel on Mr. Floyd's head and neck for close to nine minutes. Mr. Floyd repeatedly said that he could not breathe, yet Officer Chauvin showed no mercy and told Mr. Floyd to "stop talking, stop yelling. It takes a heck of a lot of oxygen to talk" (BBC News, 2020). Sadly, George Floyd knew he was going to die and said "Can't believe this man. Mom, I love you. Love you. Tell my kids I love them. I'm dead" (BBC News, 2020). Even after watching the video, there were many who willfully participated in the defamation of George Floyd and the subsequent shaming of the protests that happened following it. Unfortunately, George Floyd was a victim with minor guilt that cost him his life and his daughter to lose her father. Yet it was Officer Chauvin's complete lack of respect for another human, a **black** human, that was and still is extremely appalling and sickening.

After discussing the examples of some of the types of victims, we will move on to discuss the psychological impact that racism has on its recipients. According to the American Psychological Association (2020), trauma is an emotional response to a horrific event, such as an automobile accident, a sexual assault or rape, or a natural disaster. However, an additional horrific event that is not included in that definition is racism, which is just as traumatic or more so than some of the other examples above. When a person goes through a traumatic or perceived traumatic event, the body responds in various ways. One often goes through a state of shock and denial that the event occurred. For example, the first time I remember directly experiencing racism, I was nine and it changed my entire perception of the world. The shock of learning that some hate people simply because of their skin color was hard to understand. The absurd concept of hating solely because of a difference was far beyond my nine-year-old comprehension and still is to this day. Skin color cannot be changed. No one asks to be born, nor do they ask to be born with beautiful dark skin, yet here we are.

The longer the symptoms of trauma go untreated or unacknowledged, the more unpredictable one's reactions become. A person may experience flashbacks, anxiety or panic attacks, anger and aggression, and hypervigilance. Outwardly, some of these responses present themselves as other emotions that are easier to express, like anger and aggression. Anger covers up hurt and pain and the feelings of inadequacy due to not being able to prevent the trauma from happening. One dwells on the things that they could have and should have done to prevent the situation from happening. For example, when someone experiences trauma from a sexual assault or rape; it is common for a victim to blame themselves for being in the wrong place at the wrong time, questioning if they acted in a manner that made the perpetrator choose them, and what they could have done differently. While these thoughts are understandable, it is never the victim's fault for becoming a victim of a sexual assault or rape. Now if we take that same thought process and apply it to victims of racism, we can see that it is never the victim's fault for being the target of a racist encounter. It should also be easy to see that being a victim of this particular trauma would elicit similar emotional and psychological responses.

From personal experiences with racism, I tend to dwell on the situation and re-play it over and over in my mind. I try to think of different ways that the situation could have gone, how I could have responded better, and even why me. What did I do to this person or group of persons to feel that it is acceptable to devalue my existence on this earth? What have they done to feel that they are superior in any form to anyone else? The simple answer is that **blacks** were brought to America to be subservient. In the spirit of ignorance, laws were written that deemed a **black** as only three-fifths of a person. Another law to keep blacks in bondage was the unofficial rule that the patent system was not available to **blacks** born into slavery, as they were not considered citizens (Johnson, 2017). The United States Commissioner of Patents did make it an official rule in 1857 that inventions by slaves could not be patented (Johnson, 2017). Since the slaves were unable to apply for patents, their inventions were stolen and patented by their owners who then took credit and compensation for those inventions. Free **blacks**, on the other hand, were able to apply for patents and many of our modern-day niceties can be contributed to their ingenuity.

Much of the trauma that **blacks** go through and have gone through should have taken them out, but the mental strength, resiliency, fortitude, and sheer determination that **blacks** possess has allowed them to persevere through any and all circumstances. I do not believe that the fear of **blacks** is due to mere ignorance, but is a conscious understanding that the **black** race is powerful. The collective power is why, in my opinion, there is such a strong desire to diminish the population by murdering us in the open and then claiming that the "fear" of the superhuman, subhuman was the driving force behind the murder. Due to this innate fear of the **black** man, society in large turns a blind eye to their injustices. **Black** life is not valued by society in general, therefore, **black** life is easily extinguished without consequences for the executioners. This is the trauma of being **black.**

EPILOGUE

Sadly, the fact of the matter is that I could go on and on about the trauma that **blacks** endure, but if you are still struggling to empathize with **blacks**, then it is because you are choosing to invoke your privilege. It is absurd that we have to plead and beg to not be murdered by those who have taken a sworn oath to "protect and serve". It is even crazier that if we are murdered by said parties, we have to fight that those involved be held accountable just like anyone of us would be, yet it still does not happen.

Before 2020, it was a guessing game as to which one of our neighbors, colleagues, friends, and/or family members had racist tendencies, but this past year people revealed their true colors and feelings towards **blacks**. The callousness and hatred that has been displayed are beyond appalling and disheartening. It should go without saying that no matter the skin color, orientation, religion, or ethnicity, we are all people who bleed the same red blood. We breathe in the same oxygen and exhale carbon dioxide.

Hate only exists because it has been taught, endorsed, and excused. The excuse that one was raised to hate is unacceptable because there comes a time in life where we must make our own decisions. Now is the time to take what you have learned and make a difference. You have a decision to make: help heal the trauma that has been inflicted or choose to continue being blissfully ignorant knowing that you will never have to deal with any of these situations. That is privilege. The privilege to have a choice. Remember that you are either an ally or you are not. It is that simple.

LEARN THEIR NAMES, REMEMBER THEIR NAMES

Patrick Warren, 52, 10 Jan 21
- "Warren was shot and killed by Killeen Police Officer Reynaldo Contreras, a 5-year veteran of the department, while responding to a call concerning a man having mental health issues" (6 News Digital, 2021).

◆ ◆ ◆

Casey Goodson Jr., 23, 4 Dec 20
- Casey was shot and killed as he unlocked his door and entered his home. His death was witnessed by his 72-year-old Grandmother and two toddlers who were near the door (Walton Law, 2020).

◆ ◆ ◆

Aiden Ellison, 19, 23 Nov 20
- An argument over Ellison playing loud music in the parking lot is why he was murdered by Robert Keegan, 47 (Ramakrishnan, 2020).

◆ ◆ ◆

Quawan Charles, 15, 3 Nov 20
- A quiet 15-year-old who loved the outdoors and his dog, went missing in rural Louisiana on October 30. His body was discovered days later in a sugarcane field, 20 miles from his home; the sheriff's department told his family that the boy had drowned (Read, 2020).

Walter Wallace Jr., 27, 26 Oct 20

- "Walter Wallace Jr. should still he alive today because he was having a mental health crisis when Philadelphia police officers shot him to death" (McBride, 2020).

Jonathan Price, 31, 3 Oct 20

- "Fatally shot during an officer-involved shooting in Wolfe City while he was breaking up a fight" (Fox 4 Staff, 2020).

Dijon Kizzee, 29, 31 Aug 20

- "Los Angeles County Sheriff's deputies fatally shot Dijon Kizzee, a 29-year-old Black man, during a confrontation Monday afternoon in South LA" (Colbert, 2020)

Damian Daniels, 30, 25 Aug 20

- "a military veteran who was shot twice in the chest in front of his newly purchased home in Texas after cops were dispatched there to perform a wellness check" (Wright, 2020).

Anthony McClain, 32, 15 Aug 20

- "A father of three who was shot during a traffic stop. McClain and another man were pulled over for what police described as a vehicle code violation. " (Saucedo & Kurzweil, 2020).

◆ ◆ ◆

Julian Lewis, 60, 7 Aug 20

- "Julian Lewis went out to get a grape soda for his wife on August

7. He was pursued by a Georgia state trooper on a rural road, his car ending up pinned between a tree and the trooper's car. Lewis died after he was shot in the head" (Silverman, 2020).

Maurice Abisdid-Wagner, 30, 26 Jul 20
- "Police say Abisdid-Wagner called them to report someone was trying to break into the apartment he was staying at with a friend. According to officers, Abisdid-Wagner appeared to be having a manic episode" (KITV Web Staff).

Rayshard Brooks, 27, 12 Jun 20
- "Brooks was shot in the Wendy's parking lot Friday night after he scuffled with officers and ran away with one of their stun guns, according to the Georgia Bureau of Investigation" (Moshtaghian et al., 2020).

Priscilla Slater, 38, 10 Jun 20
- "died while in police custody at the Harper Woods Police Department" (Campbell, 2020).

Robert Forbes, 56, 6 Jun 20
- "Struck by a vehicle while demonstrating with Black Lives Matter protesters on California Avenue, dying in the hospital several days later" (Morgen, 2020).

Kamal Flowers, 24, 5 Jun 20
- "Flowers was a passenger in a Dodge Charger pulled over by Alec McKenna, a 5-year veteran of the department and another police officer. Eleven days after the fatal shooting of Kamal Flowers,

New Rochelle officials identified the police officer who shot him" (Bandler, 2020).

Jamel Floyd, 35, 3 Jun 20

- "Died after corrections officers pepper sprayed him in his cell at the Metropolitan Detention Center when he began "breaking the cell door window with a metal object," according to the federal Bureau of Prisons" (Goldberg, 2020).

David Mcatee, 52, 1 Jun 20

- "David McAtee laid in the streets of Louisville, Kentucky, for over 12 hours after being killed by law enforcement just after midnight on Sunday, May 31, amid days of protests over police violence nationwide. Noon the next day, protesters were gathered at the site. McAtee's body was still there. He was shot and killed after Louisville police and the National Guard opened fire on a crowd that had gathered at a parking lot" (Chavez, 2020).

James Scurlock, 22, 30 May 20

- "Scurlock was shot and killed as thousands of protesters swarmed the downtown Omaha and Old Market areas" (KETV Staff, 2020).

Calvin Horton Jr., 43, 27 May 20

- "John Rieple, 59, the owner of Cadillac Pawn, was arrested after he shot Horton, claiming he was a looter, according to a police source on the night of his death. Rieple was later released without charges, however. Authorities say the case remains under investigation" (Furst & Stanley, 2020).

Tony Dade, 38, 27 May 20

- "Was shot and killed by a Tallahassee police officer after allegedly stabbing to death Malik Jackson, 21, the son of a next-door neighbor. The stabbing came only hours after a group of men brutally attacked McDade in an incident caught on cell phone video" (Burlew, 2020).

Dion Johnson, 28, 25 May 20

- "Shot and killed by a Department of Public Safety trooper on Memorial Day. According to Phoenix police, Dion was parked in the gore point on the Loop 101 and Tatum Boulevard around 5:30 a.m on May 25 and was passed out. A trooper removed a gun from his car before trying to arrest him. Officers said there was a struggle and the trooper feared he would be pushed into oncoming traffic so he pulled out his gun." (Baker, 2020).

George Floyd, 46, 25 May 20

- "Officer Derek Chauvin kept his knee on Mr. Floyd's neck for at least eight minutes and 15 seconds, according to a Times analysis of timestamped video. Officer Chauvin did not remove his knee even after Mr. Floyd lost consciousness and for a full minute and 20 seconds after paramedics arrived at the scene" (Hill et al., 2020).

Maurice Gordon, 28, 23 May 20

- "A friend called a 911 dispatcher at 3:23 a.m. on May 22 and saying Gordon had just left his house "looking panicked" and saying "something about having a paranormal experience." (Hutchinson

et al., 2020)

Cornelius Fredericks, 16, 1 May 20

- "Cornelius Frederick, 16, died in a hospital two days after staff members at Lakeside Academy in Kalamazoo, which houses children in the foster care and juvenile justice systems, tackled Cornelius and restrained him for 12 minutes, allegedly for throwing a sandwich" (Kingkade, 2020).

Steven Taylor, 33, 18 Apr 20

- "San Leandro police responded to Walmart, for reports of a man brandishing a baseball bat inside. A 58-second clip shows a man — later identified as Steven Taylor, 33 — waving a bat as two officers approach him, with guns drawn. '[t]hese officers are not only poorly trained to deal with individuals suffering from a mental health crisis; their intentional and repeated application of force despite the absence of a threat" (Kelly & Hegarty, 2020).

Daniel Prude, 30, 30 Mar 20

- "Joe Prude called the police for help. His brother was acting strangely and had suddenly bolted out the back door. But when Rochester police found Daniel Prude soon after, naked and walking in the street, they handcuffed him, mocked him, put a mesh bag over his head, knelt on his back, and pushed his face into the ground until he stopped breathing, police records and body camera video show. Prude was unarmed" (O'Connor, 2020).

Breonna Taylor, 26, 13 Mar 20

- "On March 13, Taylor and her boyfriend were in bed in her apartment in Louisville's South End when police attempted to serve a search warrant on her apartment shortly after 12:30 a.m. in a series of raids related to Taylor's ex-boyfriend. They eventually used a battering ram to open the door. Taylor's boyfriend, armed with a handgun and fearing an intruder, fired one shot, and police officers returned fire, killing Taylor, who was shot eight times" (Chavez, 2020).

◆ ◆ ◆

Barry Gedeus, 27, 8 Mar 20

- " Barry Gedeus was fatally shot by a Fort Lauderdale police officer who said he believed he was the suspect in an alleged sexual assault from earlier in the day. Gedeus was riding his bike home as police were searching for the suspect. The officer believed Gedeus matched the description of the suspect, a **Black** male who has dreadlocks. He was shot 10 times" (CBS News, 2020).

◆ ◆ ◆

Manuel Ellis, 33, 3 Mar 20

- "Manuel Ellis, a 33-year-old **black** man from Tacoma, Washington, can be heard screaming, "I can't breathe" in police dispatcher audio released. The recording was made shortly before Ellis's death in police custody — and in it, he echoes the words of other **black** men who were killed during their arrests, like George Floyd and Eric Garner. Ellis was arrested in Tacoma on March 3; officers said they saw him "trying to open car doors of occupied vehicles," according to the police department. Officers also said Ellis violently confronted them first, but Sara McDowell, a witness who was in a vehicle behind the arresting officer's car, told the New York Times the police first provoked Ellis. When Ellis walked up to the police vehicle, an officer knocked him to the ground by opening the car door, she said. Videos recorded by McDowell, released on Friday, show police officers punching Ellis as he lies on the ground and telling him to put his hands behind his back" (Kim, 2020).

Ahmaud Arbery, 25, 23 Feb 20

- "Travis and Greg McMichael and a third man in another pickup, William "Roddie" Bryan, used their trucks to chase down and box in Arbery, who repeatedly reversed directions and ran into a ditch while trying to escape. Travis McMichael then got out of his truck and confronted Arbery, later telling police he shot him in self-defense after Arbery refused his order to get on the ground, GBI agent Richard Dial said. He said a close examination of the video of the shooting shows the first shot was to Arbery's chest, the second was to his hand, and the third hit his chest again before he collapsed in the road in a subdivision in the port town of Brunswick" (Bynum, 2020).

Lionel Morris, 39, 4 Feb 20

- "In the original police report, an officer said that while trying to get Morris to the ground he "pushing his head down" and that "his head inadvertently hit a shelf causing a minor laceration." That same officer also said he tased Morris in the back while he was on the ground in an attempt to gain control of his arms to arrest him. Another officer admitted to punching Morris two to four times in the back and elbow "in an attempt to gain compliance" in order to gain access to the left arm. Morris can be heard saying he "can't breathe" while an officer has a knee to his back. That officer says, "If you can talk, you can breathe." At one point, at least three officers have a foot on him while another officer puts her knee onto his should as he complains that he can't breathe" (THV11 Digital, 2020).

Jaquyn O'Neill Light, 20, 28 Jan 20

- "Jaquyn was killed after he allegedly tried to run from police on Jan. 28. Officer did not reveal that Light was not in possession of a gun. Officer Pollock's body-worn camera was not activated until after the shooting and ran for about 10 minutes" (FOX8 Digital Desk & Bargebuhr, 2020).

❖ ❖ ❖

William Green, 43, 27 Jan 20
- William was "Killed when he was shot seven times by a Maryland police officer, Cpl. Michael Owens, while sitting handcuffed in front of a police cruiser. Green was handcuffed with his arms behind his back and placed in the front seat of Owens' police cruiser. At some point, Owens got in the driver seat of the cruiser and shot Green seven times, killing him, police officials said." (Hutchinson, 2020).

❖ ❖ ❖

Darius Tarver, 23, 23 Jan 20
- "Tarver was involved in a near fatal collision shortly before he was killed where he sustained a traumatic brain injury. He was prematurely released from ICU and subsequently began to exhibit signs of significant mental impairment. On the day he was killed, he barricaded himself in his room while muttering to himself about God and light. Thus, his roommate called the police and asked for help" (CBS DFW, 2020).

❖ ❖ ❖

Miciah Lee, 18, 5 Jan 20
- "On Jan. 5, at 5:48 p.m., a 911 call was received by Sparks Police emergency dispatch from Susan Clopp, Miciah Lee's mother. She can be heard informing the dispatcher that her son was suicidal and intent upon death by either suicide or "cop. Clopp told the dispatcher she and her two other sons were attempting to block

Lee's car with their bodies, so he wouldn't leave. During the 911 call, Clopp said she worried Lee would run them over in his attempt to flee. Clopp also said Lee was mentally unstable and had a history of drug use. Video shows SPD officer Ryan Patterson shouting that Lee had a gun. Five shots—confirmed to have come from Patterson's gun—and an additional two shots can be heard in the seconds thereafter. The other two shots came from SPD officer Eric DeJesus, who'd approached Lee's vehicle on the passenger side. The .40 caliber Glock pistol Lee was carrying was not loaded, the report noted (Davis, 2020).

Sadly, these names are just the tip of the iceberg. I strongly urge you to look up each name and their alleged "crime" that resulted in a death sentence without a judge or jury.

BIBLIOGRAPHY

6 News Digital. (2021, January 14). Attorney for Patrick Warren Sr., family says Killeen officer was "hostile" and "not prepared" for mental health call. Kcentv.com. https://www.kcentv.com/article/news/local/attorney-for-patrick-warren-family-holds-press-conference-at-bell-county-courthouse/500-a9c728e3-1bd3-457f-bc31-02fc3c268573

ABC News. (2020, January 30). "One of the worst incidents in American history": Family of handcuffed man fatally shot by officer demands justice. ABC News. https://abcnews.go.com/US/worst-incidents-american-history-family-handcuffed-man-fatally/story?id=68639003

American Psychological Association. (2020). Trauma and Shock https://www.apa.org/topics/trauma

AZFamily News Staff. (2020, June 3). Video shows apparent moments after Dion Johnson was shot by DPS in Phoenix. AZFamily. https://www.azfamily.com/news/video-shows-apparent-moments-after-dion-johnson-was-shot-by-dps-in-phoenix/article_f05aeb16-a616-11ea-8048-d727ea1bb4e7.html

Bandler, J. (2020, June 16). New Rochelle police release new details on Flowers shooting, including ID of shooter. The Journal News. https://www.lohud.com/story/news/local/westchester/new-rochelle/2020/06/16/new-rochelle-police-shooting-kamal-flowers/3199895001/

BBC News. (2020, July 16). The last 30 minutes of George Floyd's life. *BBC News*. https://www.bbc.com/news/world-us-canada-52861726

Burlew, J. (2020, June 2). "I need help": McDade struggled with mental illness before fatal stabbing, police shooting. Tallahassee Democrat. https://www.tallahassee.com/story/news/local/2020/06/02/natosha-tony-mcdade-tallahasssee-protests-protest-mental-illness-fatal-stabbing-police-shooting/5300384002/

Bynum, R. (2020, June 4). Testimony: Shooter used racist slur as Arbery lay dying. AP NEWS. https://apnews.com/article/7122aaf2c54ed22590a5b8d32565a58f

Campbell, A. (2020, June 12). Family demands answers after woman dies in Harper Woods police custody. WXYZ. https://www.wxyz.com/news/region/wayne-county/family-demands-answers-after-woman-dies-in-harper-woods-police-custody

CBS DFW. (2020, March 6). Attorney: Darius Tarver Suffered "Mental Health Crisis" When He Was Killed. https://dfw.cbslocal.com/2020/03/06/attorney-darius-tarver-suffered-mental-health-crisis/

CBS News. (2020). Police in the U.S. killed 164 Black people in the first 8 months of 2020. These are their names. (Part I: January-April). Www.cbsnews.com. https://www.cbsnews.com/pictures/black-people-killed-by-police-in-the-u-s-in-2020/49/

Chávez, A. (2020, June 1). Louisville Police Left the Body of David McAtee on the Street for 12 Hours. The Intercept. https://theintercept.com/2020/06/01/louisville-police-left-the-body-of-david-mcatee-on-the-street-for-12-hours/

Chavez, N. (2020, September 24). These are the people at the center of the Breonna Taylor case. CNN. https://www.cnn.com/2020/09/23/us/breonna-taylor-case-people/index.html

Colbert, C., Gauk-Roger, T., & Mossburg, C. (2020, September 2). Fatal police shooting of Black man sparks protests in Los Angeles. CNN. https://www.cnn.com/2020/09/01/us/los-angeles-police-shooting/index.html

Davis, J. (2020, June 30). Miciah Lee's death by Sparks Police determined justified under Nevada law. This Is Reno. https://thisisreno.com/2020/06/miciah-lees-death-by-sparks-police-determined-justified-under-nevada-law/

Department of Justice. (2020, December 29). Justice Department Announces Closing of Investigation into 2014 Officer Involved Shooting in Cleveland, Ohio. Office of Public Affairs. https://www.justice.gov/opa/pr/justice-department-announces-closing-investigation-2014-officer-involved-shooting-cleveland

Drug Policy Alliance. (n.d.). *Race and the Drug War*. Drug Policy Alliance. Retrieved January 4, 2021, from https://drugpolicy.org/issues/race-and-drug-war

Equal Justice Initiative. (2017a). Lynching in America: Confronting the Legacy of Racial Terror (pp. 1–88). Equal Justice Initiative.

Equal Justice Initiative. (2017b, January 31). Emmett Till's Accuser Admits She Lied. Equal Justice Initiative. https://eji.org/news/emmett-till-accuser-admits-she-lied/

Federal Bureau of Prisons. (2021, January 2). BOP statistics: Inmate race. Bop.Gov. https://www.bop.gov/about/statistics/statistics_inmate_race.jsp

FOX 4. (2020, October 4). Family says Jonathan Price killed in Wolfe City officer-involved shooting while breaking up fight. FOX 4 News Dallas-Fort Worth; FOX 4 News Dallas-Fort Worth. https://www.fox4news.com/news/family-says-jonathan-price-killed-in-wolfe-city-officer-involved-shooting-while-breaking-up-fight

Fox 8 Digital Desk, & Bargebuhr, T. (2020, July 17). Officer shot Graham man accidentally or in self-defense, district attorney says; suspect was not armed. Myfox8.com. https://myfox8.com/news/officer-shot-graham-man-accidentally-or-in-self-defense-district-attorney-says-suspect-was-not-armed/

Furst, R., & Stanley, G. (2020, June 23). Mystery remains weeks after a pawnshop owner fatally shot a man during Minneapolis unrest. Star Tribune. https://www.startribune.com/mystery-remains-over-death-outside-pawn-shop-during-mpls-unrest/571426662/

Goldberg, N. (2020, June 30). Family of inmate who died at Brooklyn federal jail after pepper spray incident demands release of surveillance video. Nydailynews.com. https://www.nydailynews.com/new-york/ny-jamel-floyd-death-pepper-spray-20200630-o2je5bj3aja2jd375fikkk6v4q-story.html

Hill, E., Tiefenthäler, A., Triebert, C., Jordan, D., Willis, H., & Stein, R. (2020, May 31). How george floyd was killed in police custody. The New York Times. https://www.nytimes.com/2020/05/31/us/george-floyd-investigation.html

History.com Editors. (2019, June 6). *Black Panthers*. History. https://www.history.com/topics/civil-rights-movement/black-panthers

Hutchinson, B. (2019, October 2). *Death of an innocent man: Timeline of wrong-apartment murder trial of Amber Guyger*. ABC News; ABC News. https://abcnews.go.com/US/death-innocent-man-timeline-wrong-apartment-murder-trial/story?id=65938727

Hutchinson, B., Riley, D., & Wagschal, G. (2020, June 8). Dash-cam video captures struggle in fatal New Jersey shooting of black driver. ABC News. https://abcnews.go.com/US/jersey-officials-release-body-camera-video-police-killing/story?id=71130275

Johnson, S. (2017, February 15). America's always had black inventors – even when the patent system explicitly excluded them. The Conversation. https://theconversation.com/americas-always-had-black-inventors-even-when-the-patent-system-explicitly-excluded-them-72619

Kelly, G., & Hegarty, P. (2020, April 21). Family's lawyer, activists decry San Leandro police shooting. East Bay Times. https://www.eastbaytimes.com/2020/04/20/familys-lawyer-activists-decry-san-leandro-police-shooting/

KETV Staff Report. (2020, June 2). Killing of James Scurlock begins to gain national attention. KETV. https://www.ketv.com/article/killing-of-james-scurlock-begins-to-gain-national-attention/32729227

Kim, C. (2020, June 6). The fatal arrest of Manuel Ellis, another black man who yelled "I can't breathe," explained. Vox. https://www.vox.com/2020/6/6/21282483/manuel-ellis-black-man-killed-police-cant-breathe-george-floyd

Kingkade, T. (2020, July 22). Video shows tackling and fatal restraint of teen in Michigan foster facility. NBC News. https://www.nbcnews.com/news/us-news/video-shows-fatal-restraint-cornelius-fredericks-16-michigan-foster-facility-n1233122

KITV Web Staff. (2020, August 14). Man dies after arrest on Maui, body cam footage released. Www.kitv.com. https://www.kitv.com/story/42498179/man-dies-after-arrest-on-maui-body-cam-footage-released

McBride, J. (2020, October 27). Walter Wallace Jr.: Philadelphia Man Shot & Killed by Police. Heavy.com. https://heavy.com/news/walter-wallace-jr/

MedlinePlus. (2020). Mental Disorders. Medlineplus.Gov; National Library of Medicine. https://medlineplus.gov/mentaldisorders.html

Mental Health America. (n.d.). Racial Trauma. Mental Health America. Retrieved January 6, 2021, from https://www.mhanational.org/racial-trauma

Mock, B. (2015, June 11). The Origins of the Phrase "Black-on-Black Crime." Www.Bloomberg.com. https://www.bloomberg.com/news/articles/2015-06-11/examining-the-origins-of-the-phrase-black-on-black-crime

Nellis, A. (2016, June 14). The Color of Justice: Racial and Ethnic Disparity in State Prisons | The Sentencing Project. The Sentencing Project. https://www.sentencingproject.org/publications/color-of-justice-racial-and-ethnic-disparity-in-state-prisons/

Morgen, S. (2020, June 13). "Everybody cared for him": Sister of Robert Forbes, Bakersfield protester struck by car, speaks out. The Bakersfield Californian. https://www.bakersfield.com/news/everybody-cared-for-him-sister-of-robert-forbes-bakersfield-protester-struck-by-car-speaks-out/article_3f2cbfbc-ad15-11ea-a783-73509c54e646.html

Moshtaghian, A., Croft, J., Murphy, P. P., McCleary, K., & Vera, A. (2020, June). Atlanta officer who fatally shot Rayshard Brooks has been terminated. CNN. https://www.cnn.com/2020/06/13/us/atlanta-police-shooting-wendys/index.html

O'Connor, M. (2020, September 2). His Brother Called For Help After He Was Acting Strangely. Police Knelt On Him Until He Was Brain Dead. The Appeal. https://theappeal.org/daniel-prude-rochester-new-york-police-killing/

Ramakrishnan, J. (2020, November 26). Man charged with fatally shooting a 19-year-old Black man in Ashland over "loud music." OregonLive. https://www.oregonlive.com/crime/2020/11/ashland-man-charged-with-murder-after-allegedly-shooting-a-19-year-old-black-man-over-loud-music.html?outputType=amp&__twitter_impression=true

Read, B. (2020, November 24). What Happened to Quawan Charles? The Cut. https://www.thecut.com/article/quawan-charles-death-in-louisiana-what-we-know.html

SAGE Publications. (2016). *Introduction to Victimology*. SAGE Publications; https://us.sagepub.com/sites/default/files/upm-binaries/70565_Daigle_Chapter_1.pdf

Sanchez, S. (n.d.). *1.14. Victims and Victim Typologies*. Pressbooks.pub; Pressbooks. Retrieved February 3, 2021, from https://openoregon.pressbooks.pub/ccj230/chapter/1-14-victims-in-the-cj-system/

Saucedo, C., & Kurzweil, A. (2020, August 17). Crowd gathers for vigil honoring Anthony McClain, who was killed in Pasadena police shooting. KTLA. https://ktla.com/news/dozens-gather-for-demonstration-honoring-man-killed-in-pasadena-police-shooting/

Say Their Names List 2020 - #SayTheirNames. (n.d.). Say every.Name. Retrieved January 4, 2021, from https://sayevery.name/

ScienceDirect. (2014). *Victimology - an overview | ScienceDirect Topics*. Www.sciencedirect.com. https://www.sciencedirect.com/topics/social-sciences/victimology

Silverman, H. (2020, August 17). A Georgia man was fatally shot by a state trooper. His family's attorney says he was on his way to the store to get his wife a soda. CNN. https://www.cnn.com/2020/08/17/us/georgia-julian-lewis-death-family/index.html

THV11 Digital. (2020, July 29). Conway police release bodycam video after man dies in police custody. Thv11.com. https://www.thv11.com/article/news/crime/conway-police-edited-bodycam-death/91-8fd924be-5cfa-40c9-a45e-35fdfdc99def

US Census Bureau. (2019, July 1). QuickFacts: United States. Census Bureau QuickFacts; United States Census Bureau. https://www.census.gov/quickfacts/fact/table/US/PST045219

Vanden Brook, T. (2020, May 27). Air Force admits "persistent and consistent" racial bias against black airmen, records show. USA TODAY. https://www.usatoday.com/story/news/politics/2020/05/27/records-show-air-force-admits-persistent-consistent-bias-black-airmen/5179439002/

WaltonBrownLaw. (2020, December 6). Family of Casey Christopher Goodson, Jr. Demands Answers in His Death. Waltonbrownlaw.com. https://waltonbrownlaw.com/news/54b1f3718471a0e94eec7235557a487b/single/133

Wright, B. C. T. (2020, September 1). RIP Damian Daniels: Everything To Know About Military Veteran Killed By Cops During Wellness Check. NewsOne. https://newsone.com/4006593/damian-daniels-police-shooting-everything-to-know/

ACKNOWLEDGEMENTS

This book was written out of necessity. We have shouted, we have protested, we have pleaded, and we have begged for others to value our lives. I hope that when you read the list of names that you take the time to research them and learn their story to remember their names. Sadly, by the time this book is published, there may be more to add to the list. It is depressing to wake up to the news of another unarmed **black** American slain by law enforcement and so-called vigilantes. It is psychologically damaging to read the comments, see the lack of respect for **black** life, and the hatred that people have for those they have never even met. With that being said, thank you to those who have taken a firm stance in unity and proudly declare that **BLACK** LIFE MATTERS.

◆ ◆ ◆

ABOUT THE AUTHOR

Élimene Merizier is a Ph.D. candidate in Forensic Psychology specializing in Victimology at Walden University. Her extensive research on trauma, psychology, and victimology enhanced her understanding of the trauma that **black** Americans go through. Along with the educational background, she also has experienced racism in various forms both in the military and civilian life. Each incident compounds the trauma already experienced and adds to the psychological toll.

Élimene double majored in her undergrad to achieve a Bachelor of Arts degree in Criminal Justice and Bachelor of Social Work degree from Loras College in 2009 with a Minor in Sociology. After college, she served six years on Active Duty in the Air Force and is now serving part time as a Reservist. In 2017, Élimene earned her Master's degree in Forensic Psychology specializing in Community Relations from Walden University.

She currently lives in the Sunshine State near beautiful white, sandy beaches and gorgeous blue-green water and works as a Mental Health Clinician. Élimene spends her "free time" sewing, homeschooling her daughter, studying to be a Forensic Psychologist, writing, listening to music, and playing music.

www.ingramcontent.com/pod-product-compliance
Lightning Source LLC
Chambersburg PA
CBHW071240240726
48654CB00009B/1137